TONY COLEMAN
Authentic Blues Dru

T0085336

Introduction

For as long as I can remember, I always wanted to be a drummer. For me as a child, it didn't matter what type of music or artist; I just loved music and wanted to be a drummer.

Fast forward to many years of serious hard work and pursuing my goal of a professional music career. I ended up playing drums with the world's greatest blues and soul musicians and fulfilled my dreams.

In my experience of playing the blues, one of the most important things to do—after learning to play solidly, with consistency, and in time—is to learn the blues shuffle.

The shuffles that I'm about to share with you in this video and book are what made my career and the artists that I played with extremely happy.

First and foremost, I would like you to understand that what I am explaining to you in this video are not only my personal opinions. The knowledge and skills that I am sharing are based on actual experience, history of the genre, and requirements from the artists that I played and toured with. Artists such as...

B.B. King	Otis Clay	Little Joe Blue
Bobby "Blue" Bland	Charlie Musselwhite	Frankie Lee
Albert King	Matt "Guitar" Murphy	Otis Grand
Albert Collins	Luther Tucker	Z.Z. Hill
Etta James	Johnnie Taylor	Willie Clayton
Buddy Guy	Katie Webster	James Cotton
Koko Taylor	Lucky Peterson	O.V. Wright
Ike Turner	Kenny Neal	Junior Wells

And here are some of the other artists that I've played and/or recorded with...

James Brown	Waylon Jennings	Kim Wilson
Willie Nelson	Billy Gibbons	Wayne Bennett
Carlos Santana	Kenny Wayne Shepherd	Mel Brown
Ray Charles	Kris Kristofferson	Pappo
Dierks Bentley	George Duke	Davey Davies
Ron Wood	George Benson	Lee Ritenour
Robert Cray	Lowell Fulson	Mick Hucknall
The Neville Brothers	John Lee Hooker	Anson Funderburgh
Lonnie Brooks	John McLaughlin	Johnny Copeland
Slash	Ruth Brown	Shemekia Copeland
Susan Tedeschi	Irma Thomas	Rufus Thomas
The Allman Brothers	Joe Louis Walker	Kevin Brown
Derek Trucks	Stevie Ray Vaughan	And many, many more
Warren Haynes	Jimmie Vaughan	

It is my sincere hope that you enjoy this video and book and use these principles and exercises to correctly play this often misunderstood and overlooked skill of the authentic blues shuffle.

— Tony Coleman

ABOUT THE VIDEO

To download or stream the video files, simply go to **www.halleonard.com/mylibrary** and enter the code found on page 1 of this book.

The book features detailed drum notation for select video examples. The timecode shown at the start of each written example indicates exactly where it is demonstrated in the video.

DRUM LEGEND

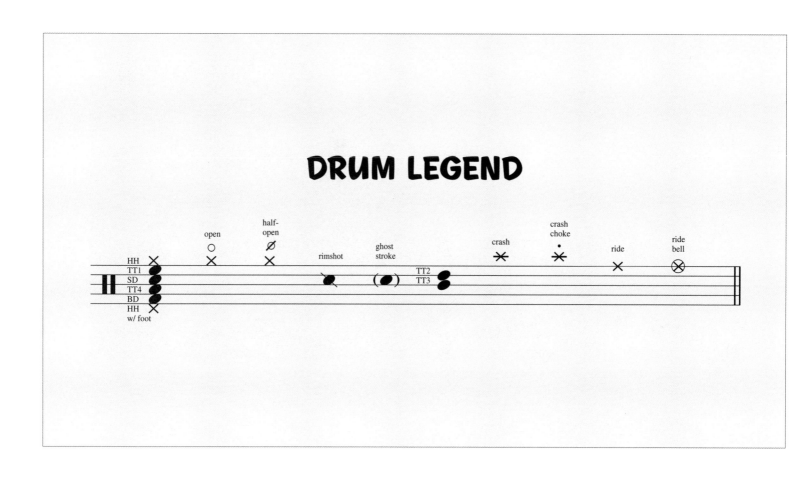

BASIC SHUFFLE

Basic Shuffle `0:04`

Basic Shuffle variation 1 `2:45`

Basic Shuffle variation 2 `3:40`

Basic Shuffle variation 3 `4:06`

Basic Shuffle variation 4 `5:27`

(rimshot snare on 2 & 4)

GOSPEL SHUFFLE

Gospel Shuffle 0:53

Gospel Shuffle variation 1:22

DOUBLE SHUFFLE

Double Shuffle `0:27`

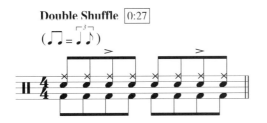

Double Shuffle variation `1:21`

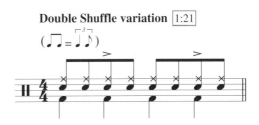

TEXAS SHUFFLE

Texas Shuffle `0:47`

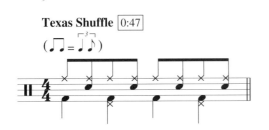

Texas Shuffle variation `1:22`

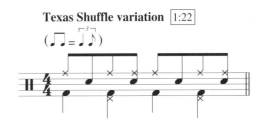

KANSAS CITY SHUFFLE

Kansas City Shuffle `0:49`

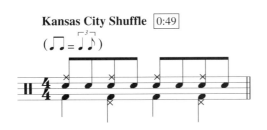

Kansas City Shuffle variation `1:00`

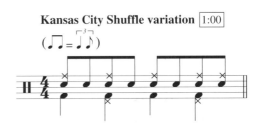

SLOW BLUES

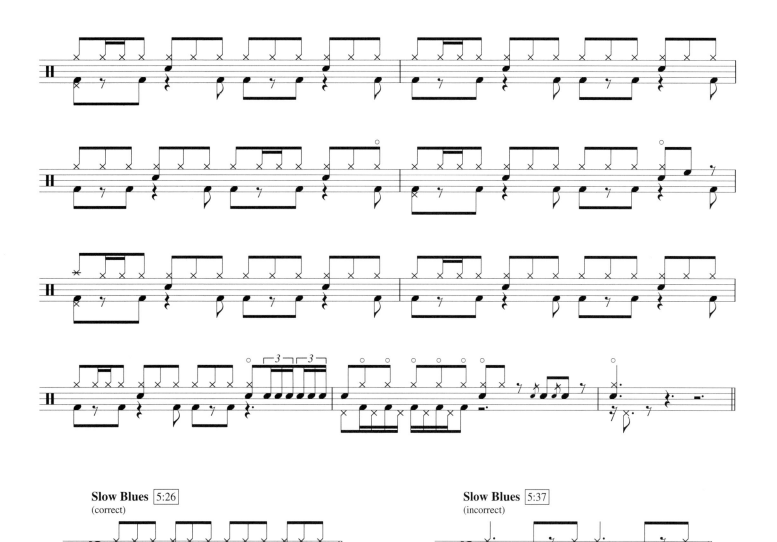

Slow Blues 5:26
(correct)

Slow Blues 5:37
(incorrect)

BLUES FUNK

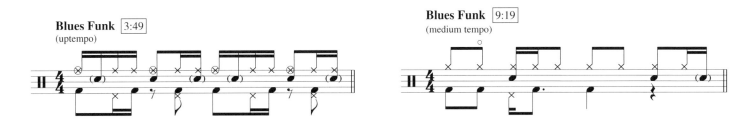

MODULATE UP FILLS

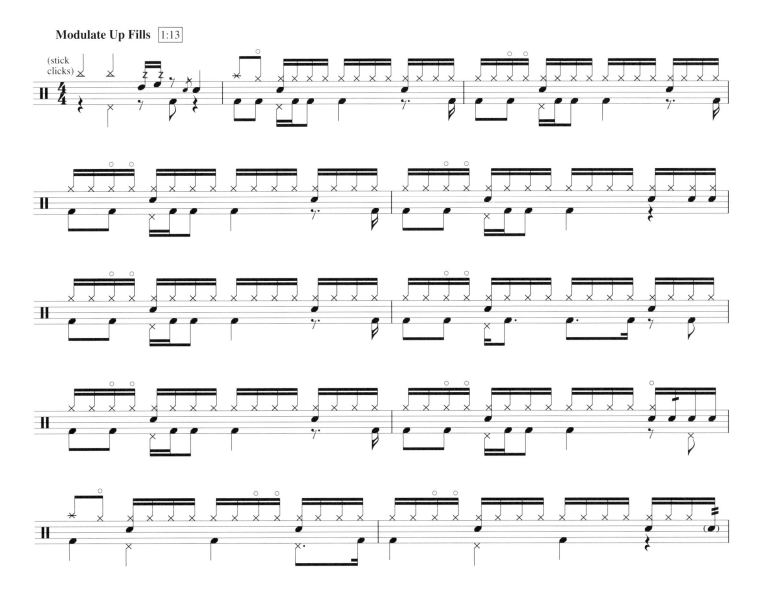

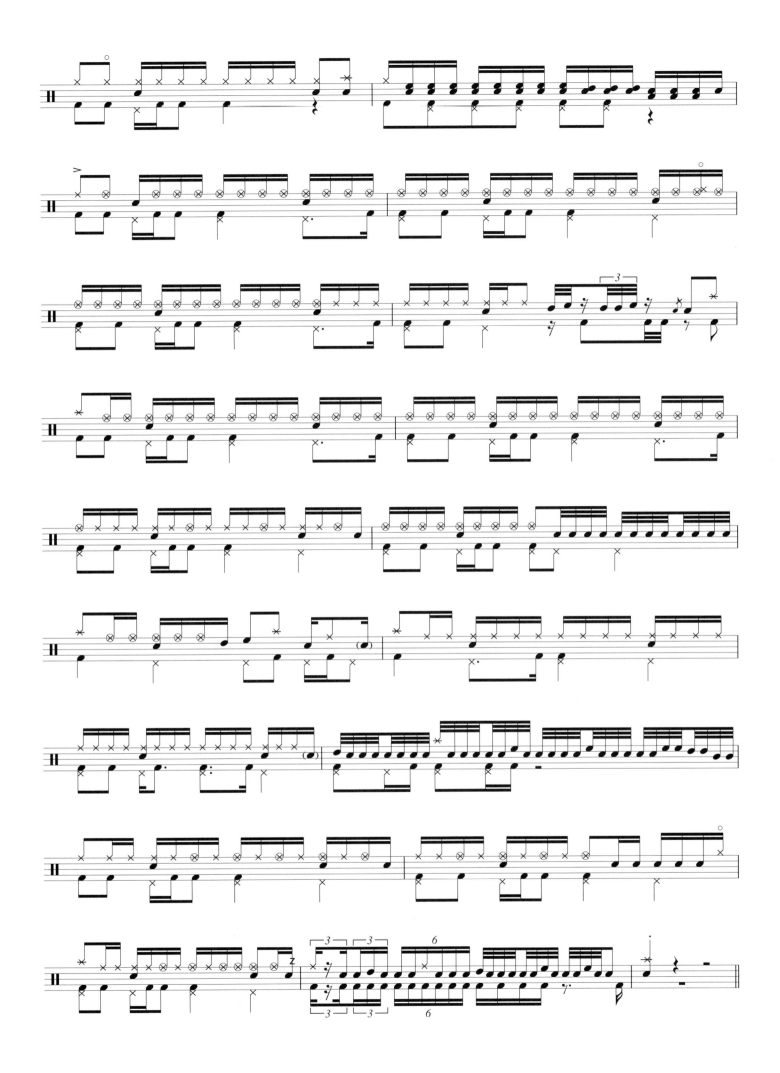

INTROS AND ENDINGS

OUTRO

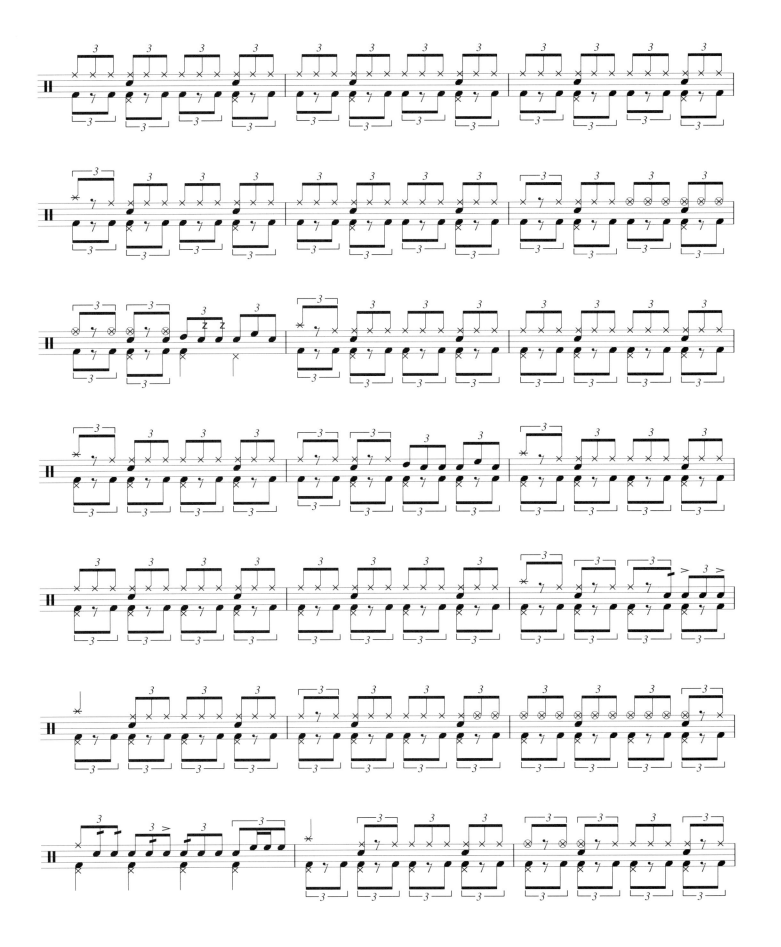

14

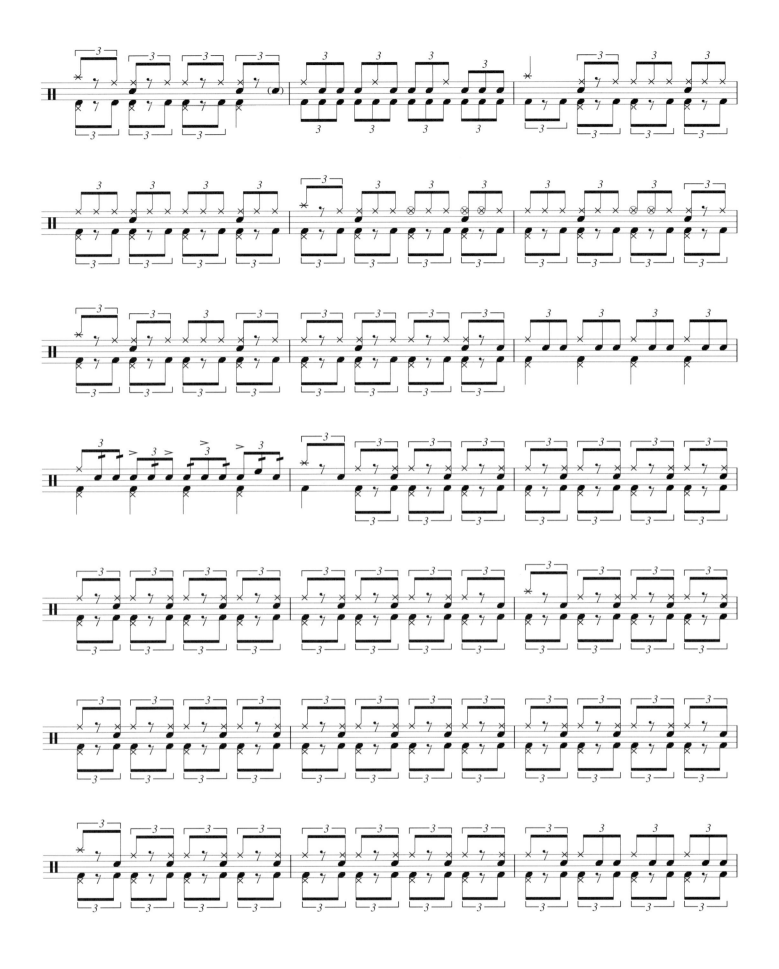